P(

NIETZSCHE: DITH   ᴧ DIONYSUS

FRIEDRICH NIETZSCHE

Dithyrambs of Dionysus

(DIONYSOS-DITHYRAMBEN)

TRANSLATED WITH AN INTRODUCTION
AND NOTES BY R.J. HOLLINGDALE

ANVIL PRESS POETRY

This edition published in 2001
by Anvil Press Poetry Ltd
Neptune House 70 Royal Hill London SE10 8RF
First published in 1984

ISBN 0 85646 327 2

This book is published
with financial assistance from
The Arts Council of England

A catalogue record for this book
is available from the British Library

Designed and set in Monotype Ehrhardt by Anvil
Printed and bound in England
by Cromwell Press, Trowbridge, Wiltshire

Contents

Introduction

Friedrich Nietzsche was born in 1844 and produced the philo-
sophical writings on which his claim to attention mainly rests
during the 1870s and 1880s; in 1889 he suffered a mental break-
down which terminated his productivity, and he died in 1900.
His reputation, which now stands higher than it has ever done
before, is that of a thinker whose insights and influence mark a
new stage in the progress of Western thought, and it is now
normal to rank him with Marx and Freud as one of the creators
of the twentieth century; his earliest reputation, however,
which he acquired during the 1890s, was that of a German
philosopher who, very surprisingly, wrote poetry.

He began writing poetry, in fact, when he was still a boy,
well before he had any interest in matters that could be called,
even in a juvenile sense, philosophical. His attempts at verse
were paralleled by attempts at musical composition, and until
about 1860 his whole development seemed to be that of a
potential "artist" of some sort. Composition was, in the end,
never more than a hobby (at bottom no more than an extension
of improvising at the piano); but to the writing of poetry he
gave from the first the kind of attention that could be called
professional: he appears to have realized that, while the content
of what he wrote at the age of fifteen could be only derivative
and juvenile, this would later on take care of itself if only he
was able to master the technique of writing in verse. He applied
himself to this with genuine dedication and produced a body of
"juvenilia" whose subject-matter is conventional and uninter-
esting but which shows a steady advance in technical ability that
is clearly the consequence of deliberate application and practice.
He then continued to write poetry, in a large range of styles, for
the remainder of his active life.

Most of the verse he wished to preserve he published
within the framework of his philosophical works, the only
exceptions being the collection *Idyllen aus Messina* (1882),

which appeared in a magazine, and the *Dionysos-Dithyramben*. The earliest large selection of his poems, published and hitherto unpublished, appeared in 1898 under the title *Gedichte und Sprüche*.

2

Nietzsche's mature poetry is of four distinct kinds. Firstly, there are the brief, rhymed epigrammatic pieces: they make a single point in the fewest possible words, and are in essence a manifestation of the pleasure he always took in expressing himself aphoristically. "My ambition", he wrote in *Twilight of the Idols*, "is to say in ten sentences what everyone else says in a book – what everyone else *does not* say in a book"; and an "un-German" conciseness and *presto* is a general characteristic of his style even when he is not writing aphoristically. Here are some examples.

FÜR TÄNZER

Glattes Eis
Ein Paradeis
Für den, der gut zu tanzen weiß.

For Dancers   Slippery ice [is] a paradise for him who knows how to dance well.

MEINE HÄRTE

Ich muß weg über hundert Stufen,
Ich muß empor und hör euch rufen:
"Hart bist du! Sind wir denn von Stein?" –
Ich muß weg über hundert Stufen,
Und niemand möchte Stufe sein.

My Kind of Hardness   I have to pass over a hundred steps, I have to go up and I hear you cry: "How hard you are! Do you think we're made of stone?" I have to pass over a hundred steps, and no one wants to be a step.

DER NÄCHSTE

Nah hab den Nächsten ich nicht gerne:
Fort mit ihm in die Höh und Ferne!
Wie würd er sonst zu meinem Sterne? –

My Neighbour I don't like my neighbour near me. Away with him into distant heights! How otherwise could he become my star?

Wer viel einst zu verkünden hat,
schweigt viel in sich hinein:
Wer einst den Blitz zu zünden hat,
muß lange – Wolke sein.

He who has much to proclaim one day, stays silently much immersed within himself: he who has to kindle the lightning one day, must for a long time – be a cloud.

Then there are the poems of more conventional length and subject whose most obvious model is the briefer poems of Heinrich Heine, of whom Nietzsche was an unqualified admirer ("The highest conception of the lyric poet was given me by *Heinrich Heine* . . . He possessed that divine malice without which I cannot imagine perfection . . . It will one day be said that Heine and I have been by far the first artists of the German language." – *Ecce Homo*):

Dorthin – *will* ich; und ich traue
Mir fortan und meinem Griff.
Offen liegt das Meer, ins Blaue
Treibt mein Genueser Schiff.

Alles glänzt mir neu und neuer,
Mittag schläft auf Raum und Zeit – :
Nur *dein* Auge – ungeheuer
Blickt michs an, Unendlichkeit!

I *will* away – and henceforth I trust in myself and in my own hands. Open lies the sea, my Genoese ship surges onward into the blue. Everything glitters new and newer, noontide sleeps on space and time: your eye alone – dreadfully it gazes upon me, infinity!)

Thirdly, and among the best known, are the experiments in rhythmic effects:

> Mistral-Wind, du Wolken-Jäger,
> Trübsal-Mörder, Himmels-Feger,
> Brausender, wie lieb ich dich!
> Sind wir zwei nicht eines Schoßes
> Erstlingsgabe, eines Loses
> Vorbestimmte ewiglich?

Mistral wind, you hunter of clouds, killer of affliction, scourer of the skies, blusterer, how I love you! Are we two not the first fruit of one womb, eternally predestined for one fate?
>   ["An den Mistral", opening stanza]

> Ja! Ich weiß, woher ich stamme!
> Ungesättigt gleich der Flamme
> Glühe und verzehr ich mich.
> Licht wird alles, was ich fasse,
> Kohle alles, was ich lasse:
> Flamme bin ich sicherlich.

Yes, I know whence I have sprung! Insatiable as a flame I burn and consume myself. Whatever I seize hold on becomes light, whatever I leave, ashes: certainly I am a flame.
>   ["Ecce homo"]

Lastly, in point both of time and poetic intensity, we have the free, "dithyrambic" verse of which the collection *Dithyrambs of Dionysus* is the final form.

3

The *Dithyrambs of Dionysus*, in the precise shape in which we have it, is among Nietzsche's last productions and for that reason is usually accounted one of the "Werke des Zusammenbruchs" – the works of the final quarter of 1888 during which his mental breakdown of the beginning of 1889 was palpably preparing itself (the other "Werke des Zusammenbruchs" are *The Anti-Christ, Ecce Homo* and *Nietzsche contra Wagner*). The nine poems which constitute the collection were composed over the six-year period 1883–88; in the summer of 1888 Nietzsche collected them together into their present form and made fair copies of them with the clear intention of having them printed, but in the event held them back from publication until the very end of the year. On 1 January 1889 he added the dedication which prefaces the collection: they are probably the last words he wrote before he suffered, two days later, the breakdown which rendered him incapable of further rational thought. The accepted date of his mental collapse is 3 January 1889; but Nietzsche had been in a condition of pathological euphoria for the preceding three months at least and there is no question but that by the turn of the year he was already experiencing difficulty in ordering his thoughts rationally. The brief foreword to *Nietzsche contra Wagner*, for instance, which is dated "Christmas 1888", ends with three sentences which, though rational in themselves, have no obvious connection with what has gone before or with the subject of the book. It is a similar apparent disconnectedness – "apparent" because, of course, a connection does exist, though it is not a rational one – that characterizes the relationship between this dedication and the collection of poems which follows it. Except for his first book, *The Birth of Tragedy*, which is dedicated to Wagner, and the first edition of *Human, All Too Human*, which is dedicated "to the memory of Voltaire", none of Nietzsche's books bears a dedication, so that the presence of a dedication here is in itself abnormal. What is harder still to understand, however, is the identity of the dedicatee: the "poet of Isoline", Catulle Mendès, is one of the last of Nietzsche's contemporaries with whom you would think he felt any affinity; remembered today, if he is remembered at all, mainly as a leading Parisian ally and advocate of Wagner, and possibly as the author of *Le Roi Vierge*, a novel satirizing the world of Ludwig II of Bavaria and those, including Wagner, who belonged to it, Mendès seems quite out of place in the company of the *Dithyrambs of Dionysus* and Nietzsche's professed admiration for him inexplicable. (Except for the fact that both Mendès and Nietzsche had been personally acquainted with Wagner, I can discover no biographical connection between the two.) Here we are already close to the region of the irrational into which Nietzsche entered wholly on 3 January, and it is a perception of this fact that has led editors of the *Dionysos-Dithyramben* to omit the dedication to Catulle Mendès: it is first included in the edition of Karl Schlechta (*Werke in drei Bänden*, vol. 2, 1955), which I follow. Having printed it, however, it is probably all the more necessary for me to emphasize that the nine poems are *not* products of the last quarter of 1888 but of an indeterminate though certainly much longer period, and that anyone who sought in them signs of "insanity" would be looking in the wrong place.

4

Movement towards free verse was inherent in Nietzsche's prose style – or, better, in one of several prose styles which succeeded or accompanied one another during the course of his development – from the time of *Human, All Too Human* (published in 1878) onwards, when the derivative, rather heavyweight nineteenth-century German in which he had hitherto written gave way principally to a manner both older (recalling the lighter hand of the eighteenth century) and more modern (especially in its simplification of syntax and livelier tempo). Here is an example of it:

> It is probable that the objects of the religious, moral and aesthetic sensations belong only to the surface of things, while man likes to believe that here at least he is in touch with the world's heart; the reason he deludes himself is that these

things produce in him such profound happiness and unhappiness, and thus he exhibits here the same pride as in the case of astrology. For astrology believes that the starry firmament revolves around the fate of man; the moral man, however, supposes that what he has essentially at heart must also constitute the essence and heart of things.

[*Human, All Too Human 4*]

But at the same time as he was writing in this clean, objective manner, he also found satisfaction in a style of extended metaphor which brings to mind all too vividly that of the "model essay" whose defining characteristic is that it expresses a single, simple idea in as florid, far-fetched, wordy and "poetic" a manner as the writer can achieve. Here is an example:

> *In the desert of science.* – To the man of science on his unassuming and laborious travels, which must often enough be journeys through the desert, there appear those glittering mirages called "philosophical systems": with bewitching deceptive power they show the solution of all enigmas and the freshest draught of the true water of life to be near at hand; his heart rejoices, and it seems to the weary traveller that his lips already touch the goal of all the perseverance and sorrows of the scientific life, so that he involuntarily presses forward. There are other natures, to be sure, which stand still, as if bewildered by the fair illusion: the desert swallows them up and they are dead to science. Other natures again, which have often before experienced this subjective solace, may well grow exceedingly ill-humoured and curse the salty taste which these apparitions leave behind in the mouth and from which arises a raging thirst – without one having been brought so much as a single step nearer to any kind of spring.

[*Assorted Opinions and Maxims* 31]

In his case, however, the style of this passage and others like it is no more than a first, relatively primitive stage in the development of the style of *compressed* metaphor in which much of *Thus Spoke Zarathustra* (1883–85) is written:

Life is a fountain of delight; but where the rabble also drinks all wells are poisoned. . . . Many a one who went into the desert and suffered thirst with beasts of prey merely did not wish to sit around the cistern with dirty camel-drivers. . . . Here, in the extremest height, the fountain of delight gushes up for me! And here there is a life at which no rabble drinks with me! . . . Gone is the lingering affliction of my spring! Gone the malice of my snowflakes in June! Summer have I become entirely, and summer-noonday!

Rewritten in the style of "In the desert of science", this passage from *Zarathustra* would be extended to several pages; and the latter is in turn only a stage towards a style even more compressed in which almost every statement is metaphorical, and thus has in a sense to be interpreted before it can be understood, yet acts with the directness of impact normally attainable only by plain prose (i.e. prose whose implications are all on the surface):

Let us look one another in the face. We are Hyperboreans – we know well enough how much out of the way we live. "Neither by land nor by sea shalt thou find the road to the Hyperboreans": Pindar already knew that of us. Beyond the North, beyond the ice, beyond death – *our* life, *our* happiness . . . We have discovered happiness, we know the road, we have found the exit out of whole millennia of labyrinth. Who *else* has found it? – Modern man perhaps? – "I know not which way to turn; I am everything that knows not which way to turn" – sighs modern man. . . . It was from *this* modernity that we were ill – from lazy peace, from cowardly compromise, from the whole virtuous uncleanliness of modern Yes and No. This tolerance and *largeur* of heart which "forgives" everything because it "understands" everything is sirocco to us. Better to live among ice than among modern virtues and other south winds! . . . We were brave enough, we spared neither ourselves nor others: but for long we did not know *where* to apply our courage. We became gloomy, we were called fatalists. *Our* fatality – was the plenitude, the tension, the blocking-up of our forces. We thirsted for lightning and action, of all things we kept ourselves furthest from the happiness of the weaklings, from "resignation". . . . . There was a thunderstorm in our air, the nature which we are grew dark – *for we had no road.* Formula of our happiness: a Yes, a No, a straight line, a *goal.* . . .

[*The Anti-Christ* 1]

In a passage such as this the distinction between "prose" and "poetry" has been narrowed to a merely technical one; and if a kind of poetry is envisaged – a kind usually called "free verse" – of which the only regulator is cadence, then there are many passages in Nietzsche's writings (principally though not only in *Zarathustra*) where all distinction between prose and poetry has disappeared:

> Allein bin ich wieder und will es sein, allein mit reinem Himmel und freiem Meere; und wieder ist Nachmittag um mich.

> Allein bin ich wieder
> und will es sein,
> allein mit reinem Himmel
> und freiem Meere;
> und wieder ist Nachmittag um mich.

> I am again alone and willingly so, alone with the pure sky and the open sea; and again it is afternoon around me.

[*Zarathustra* III, Von der Seligkeit wider Willen]

Strongly cadenced prose and the style of compressed metaphor combined together define the "free verse" style of the *Dithyrambs of Dionysus.*

5

Nietzsche's posthumously published notebooks contain many book-titles for which there are no corresponding books; and several of his published books received their final titles only after several provisional titles had been rejected. It is therefore not in itself surprising to find that the *Dithyrambs of Dionysus* too bore many other names before this name was settled upon. We can perhaps congratulate ourselves that "Songs of the Heights. Dedicated to all Men of the Future. By a Prophet" fell out of favour; and that the same fate befell "Dionysian Songs of a Prophet", "The Mirror of Prophecy" and "The Grave of God". Other rejected titles include "To the Higher Men. Proclamations" and "Midday and Eternity". The name of Zarathustra, Nietzsche's *alter ego*, appears in "The Eternal Recurrence. Zarathustra's Dances and Festivities", "The Songs of Zarathustra. Part One: The Path to Greatness" and "Zarathustra's Songs. Out of Seven Solitudes"; and it is probably a misunderstanding which has led some students of Nietzsche to suppose that the fourth part of *Thus Spoke Zarathustra* was at one time intended to bear the title "The Temptation of Zarathustra", since it seems more likely that this title too was in fact intended for the present book. Most of these titles exhibit an excessive, sometimes comic grandiloquence: yet the title Nietzsche finally affixed is, when correctly understood, more grandiloquent than any of them.

A dithyramb is, in its primary meaning, a Greek choric hymn to Dionysus; by extension it comes to mean any Dionysian, or "Bacchanalian", hymn or poem. For Nietzsche, however, the word had acquired a larger meaning. In *The Birth of Tragedy* of 1872 he had tried to show that Greek tragedy, and thus the art of drama as such, originated in the ritual worship of Dionysus – in the dithyramb, in fact, in its original signification: the "chorus" of Greek tragedy as we have it is, he says, the "womb of the entire so-called dialogue, i.e. the entire world of the stage, of the actual drama". He proposes that drama was born out of the dithyramb in a manner analogous to the birth of lyric out of epic poetry: in the latter case the poet, invisible in the epic, emerges from it and makes himself the centre and subject of the poem; in the former the god materializes out of the throng of his worshippers. "It is an unimpeachable tradition that Greek tragedy in its oldest form depicted only the sufferings of Dionysus", he says, but goes on to assert that "Dionysus never ceased to be the tragic hero. . . . all the famous figures of the Greek stage . . . are only masks of that original

THEN ALL TRAGEDY IS ABOUT UNFETTERED POWER OF ORCHESTRA. NEO CUE VS THE CONTRACTS OF APOLLO THAT GNAWS SOCIETY

hero Dionysus." It is for this reason that he alludes to the Greek tragedian as the "Dionysian dramatist", a figure whom, in *Richard Wagner in Bayreuth* (published in 1876), he feels entitled to call the happiest of men and the one most beneficial to other men. Later and possibly better known formulations of what he means by a "dithyramb" are in their essence no more than a repetition of this original assertion that the dithyramb is the language in which Dionysus speaks for and of himself.

To the question who "Dionysus" is there are two answers. One is that he is a Greek god, and we shall take a look at this idea of him when discussing the one poem in this collection in which he appears (see Notes, p. 91). The other is that he is the force of life itself and that which, evolving out of it, controls it. In *The Birth of Tragedy*, Dionysus is visualized both historically, as the object of a religious cult, and as an ideogram for the "uncivilized" energies for which the Dionysian rites were a release. At this stage, the force which civilizes these energies and bestows form upon them is called Apollo, and Greek tragedy is described as Apollo's harnessing of Dionysus. But it was a description with which Nietzsche was not satisfied for very long, since, while "Dionysus" was plainly "given" as a phenomenon whose existence was unquestionable, the origin, even the possibility of "Apollo" was unexplained. Whence comes the force which constrains and employs – "civilizes" – man's animal nature? To ask the question in that way exposes the presupposition behind it that there exists a dualism in nature; and Nietzsche's dissatisfaction with *The Birth of Tragedy* was rooted finally in a realization that he had assumed this without reflecting at all deeply upon its implications. Ultimately, "nature" must mean everything that exists or it must be one element of a dualism whose other element has to be something outside and beyond nature, and that something can be thought of only as God; but if, as Nietzsche did, one comes to find the idea of God untenable, then all the effects observed in nature must be produced by nature itself: in the language of *The Birth of Tragedy*, the force which harnesses Dionysus must also be Dionysus. The concept of "sublimation" thus became a necessary and key concept in Nietzsche's monistic philosophy of "will to power": his attempt to show that all the phenomena of human life are expressions of one basic drive at various levels of its sublimation. Within this system of thinking, "Dionysus" becomes an ideogram for sublimated will to power, and the "Dionysian man" is now a synonym for *Übermensch*, the man in whom will to power has been sublimated into self-mastery and self-creativity.

6

The text of the *Dionysos-Dithyramben* printed here is that contained in the second volume of Nietzsche's *Werke in drei Bänden* edited by Karl Schlechta (1955). The collection was first published in 1891 together with the first public printing of Part Four of *Thus Spoke Zarathustra*; Schlechta's edition follows the texts reprinted in volume 8 of the *Gesamtausgabe in Grossoktav* (1919).

R. J. HOLLINGDALE

Dithyrambs of Dionysus

Dionysos-Dithyramben

Dionysos-Dithyramben

Indem ich der Menschheit eine unbegrenzte Wohltat erweisen will, gebe ich ihr meine Dithyramben.

Ich lege sie in die Hände des Dichters der Isoline, des größten und ersten Satyr, der heute lebt – und nicht nur heute . . .

DIONYSOS

Dithyrambs of Dionysus

In as much as I want to do mankind a boundless favour, I give them my dithyrambs.

I place them in the hands of the poet of Isoline, the first and greatest satyr alive today – and not only today . . .

DIONYSUS

Nur Narr! Nur Dichter!

Bei abgehellter Luft,
wenn schon des Taus Tröstung
zur Erde niederquillt,
unsichtbar, auch ungehört
– denn zartes Schuhwerk trägt
der Tröster Tau gleich allen Trostmilden –
gedenkst du da, gedenkst du, heißes Herz,
wie einst du durstetest,
nach himmlischen Tränen und Taugeträufel
versengt und müde durstetest,
dieweil auf gelben Graspfaden
boshaft abendliche Sonnenblicke
durch schwarze Bäume um dich liefen,
blendende Sonnen-Glutblicke, schadenfrohe.

"Der *Wahrheit* Freier – du?" so höhnten sie –
"Nein! nur ein Dichter!
ein Tier, ein listiges, raubendes, schleichendes,
das lügen muß,
das wissentlich, willentlich lügen muß,
nach Beute lüstern,
bunt verlarvt,
sich selbst zur Larve,
sich selbst zur Beute,
das – der Wahrheit Freier? . . .

Nur Narr! nur Dichter!
Nur Buntes redend,
aus Narrenlarven bunt herausredend,
herumsteigend auf lügnerischen Wortbrücken,
auf Lügen-Regenbogen

Only a Fool! Only a Poet!

When the air grows clear,
when the dew's comfort already
rains down upon the earth,
invisible and unheard
– for dew the comforter
wears tender shoes like all that gently comforts –
do you then remember, do you, hot heart,
how once you thirsted
for heavenly tears and dew showers,
thirsted, scorched and weary,
while on yellow grassy paths
wicked evening eyes of sunlight
ran about you through dark trees,
blinding, glowing sunlight-glances, malicious?

"The wooer of *truth*? – you?" so they jeered –
"No! only a poet!
an animal, cunning, preying, creeping,
that has to lie,
that knowingly, wilfully has to lie,
lusting for prey,
gaudily masked,
a mask to itself,
a prey to itself –
that – the wooer of truth? . . .

Only a fool! Only a poet!
Talking only gaudy nonsense,
gaudy nonsense from a fool's mask,
climbing around on deceitful word-bridges,
on mirage rainbows,

zwischen falschen Himmeln
herumschweifend, herumschleichend –
nur Narr! *nur* Dichter! . . .

Das – der Wahrheit Freier? . . .
Nicht still, starr, glatt, kalt,
zum Bilde worden,
zur Gottes-Säule,
nicht aufgestellt vor Tempeln,
eines Gottes Türwart:
nein! feindselig solchen Tugend-Standbildern,
in jeder Wildnis heimischer als in Tempeln,
voll Katzen-Mutwillens
durch jedes Fenster springend
husch! in jeden Zufall,
jedem Urwalde zuschnüffelnd,
daß du in Urwäldern
unter buntzottigen Raubtieren
sündlich gesund und schön und bunt liefest,
mit lüsternen Lefzen,
selig-höhnisch, selig-höllisch, selig-blutgierig,
raubend, schleichend, *lügend* liefest . . .

Oder dem Adler gleich, der lange,
lange starr in Abgründe blickt,
in *seine* Abgründe . . .
– o wie sie sich hier hinab,
hinunter, hinein,
in immer tiefere Tiefen ringeln! –

Dann,
plötzlich,
geraden Flugs,
gezückten Zugs

between false skies,
hovering, creeping –
only a fool! *only* a poet! . . .

That – the wooer of truth? . . .
Not still, stiff, smooth, cold,
become an image,
become a god's statue,
not set up before temples,
a god's watchman:
no! enemy to such statues of truth,
more at home in any wilderness than in temples,
full of cat's wantonness,
leaping through every window,
swiftly! into every chance,
sniffing out every jungle,
that you may run,
sinfully healthy and gaudy and fair,
in jungles among gaudy-speckled beasts of prey,
run with lustful lips,
happily jeering, happily hellish, happily blood-thirsty,
preying, creeping, *lying* . . .

Or like the eagle staring
long, long into abysses,
into its own abysses . . .
– oh how they circle down,
under and in,
into ever deeper depths! –

Then,
suddenly,
with straight aim,
quivering flight,

auf *Lämmer* stoßen,
jach hinab, heißhungrig,
nach Lämmern lüstern,
gram allen Lamms-Seelen,
grimmig gram allem, was blickt
tugendhaft, schafmässig, krauswollig,
dumm, mit Lammsmilch-Wohlwollen . . .

Also
adlerhaft, pantherhaft
sind des Dichters Sehnsüchte,
sind *deine* Sehnsüchte unter tausend Larven,
du Narr! du Dichter! . . .

Der du den Menschen schautest
so *Gott* als *Schaf* – ,
den Gott *zerreißen* im Menschen
wie das Schaf im Menschen
und zerreißend *lachen* –

das, das ist deine Seligkeit,
eines Panthers und Adlers Seligkeit,
eines Dichters und Narren Seligkeit!" . . .

Bei abgehellter Luft,
wenn schon des Monds Sichel
grün zwischen Purpurröten
und neidisch hinschleicht,
– dem Tage feind,
mit jedem Schritte heimlich
an Rosen-Hängematten
hinsichelnd, bis sie sinken,
nachtabwärts blaß hinabsinken:

they pounce on *lambs*,
headlong down, ravenous,
lusting for lambs,
angry at all lamb-souls,
fiercely angry at all that looks
virtuous, sheepish, curly-woolled,
stupid with lamb's milk kindliness . . .

Thus,
eaglelike, pantherlike,
are the poet's desires,
are *your* desires under a thousand masks,
you fool! you poet! . . .

You who saw man
as *god* and *sheep* –
to *rend* the god in man
as the sheep in man,
and rending *to laugh* –

that, that is your blessedness,
a panther's and eagle's blessedness,
a poet's and a fool's blessedness!" . . .

When the air grows clear,
when the moon's sickle already
creeps along, green,
envious, in the purple twilight,
– enemy to day,
with every step secretly
sickling down the hanging rose-gardens,
until they sink, sink down,
pale, down to night:

so sank ich selber einstmals
aus meinem Wahrheits-Wahnsinne,
aus meinen Tages-Sehnsüchten,
des Tages müde, krank vom Lichte,
– sank abwärts, abendwärts, schattenwärts,
von einer Wahrheit
verbrannt und durstig
– gedenkst du noch, gedenkst du, heißes Herz,
wie da du durstetest? –
daß ich verbannt sei
von aller Wahrheit!
Nur Narr! *Nur* Dichter! . . .

so I myself sank once
from my delusion of truth,
from my daytime longings,
weary of day, sick with light
– sank downwards, down to evening, down to shadows,
scorched and thirsty
with one truth
– do you remember, do you, hot heart,
how you thirsted then? –
that I am banished
from all truth!
Only a fool! *Only* a poet! . . .

Die Wüste wächst: weh dem,
der Wüsten birgt . . .

Ha!
Feierlich!
ein würdiger Anfang!
afrikanisch feierlich!
eines Löwen würdig
oder eines moralischen Brüllaffen . . .
– aber nichts für euch,
ihr allerliebsten Freundinnen,
zu deren Füßen mir,
einem Europäer unter Palmen,
zu sitzen vergönnt ist. Sela.

Wunderbar wahrlich!
Da sitze ich nun,
der Wüste nahe und bereits
so ferne wieder der Wüste,
auch in nichts noch verwüstet:
nämlich hinabgeschluckt
von dieser kleinen Oasis
– sie sperrte gerade gähnend
ihr liebliches Maul auf,
das wohlriechendste aller Mäulchen:
da fiel ich hinein,
hinab, hindurch – unter euch,
ihr allerliebsten Freundinnen! Sela.

Heil, Heil jenem Walfische,
wenn er also es seinem Gaste
wohlsein ließ! – ihr versteht
meine gelehrte Anspielung? . . .

The Desert Grows: Woe to Him
Who Harbours Deserts . . .

Ha!
Solemnly!
a worthy beginning!
solemn in an African way!
worthy of a lion
or of a moral screech-ape . . .
– but it is not for you,
you dearest maidens,
at whose feet I,
a European among palm-trees,
am permitted to sit. Selah.

Wonderful, truly!
Here I now sit,
beside the desert, and
yet so far from the desert,
and not at all devastated:
for I am swallowed down
by this little oasis
– it simply opened, yawning,
its sweetest mouth,
the sweetest-smelling of all little mouths:
then I fell in,
down, straight through – among you,
you dearest maidens! Selah.

All hail to that whale
if it made things so pleasant
for its guest! – you understand
my learned allusion? . . .

Heil seinem Bauche,
wenn es also
ein so lieblicher Oasis-Bauch war,
gleich diesem: was ich aber in Zweifel ziehe.
Dafür komme ich aus Europa,
das zweifelsüchtiger ist als alle Eheweibchen.
Möge Gott es bessern!
Amen.

Da sitze ich nun,
in dieser kleinsten Oasis,
einer Dattel gleich,
braun, durchsüßt, goldschwürig,
lüstern nach einem runden Mädchen-Maule,
mehr aber noch nach mädchenhaften
eiskalten schneeweißen schneidigen
Beißzähnen: nach denen nämlich
lechzt das Herz allen heißen Datteln. Sela.

Den genannten Südfrüchten
ähnlich, allzuähnlich
liege ich hier, von kleinen
Flügelkäfern
umtänzelt und umspielt,
insgleichen von noch kleineren
törichteren boshafteren
Wünschen und Einfällen, –
umlagert von euch,
ihr stummen, ihr ahnungsvollen
Mädchen-Katzen
Dudu und Suleika
– *umsphinxt*, daß ich in ein Wort
viel Gefühle stopfe

All hail to its belly
if it was
as sweet an oasis-belly
as this is: which, however, I call in question.
Since I come from Europe,
which is more sceptical than any little wife.
May God improve it!
Amen.

Here I sit now
in this smallest oasis
like a date,
brown, sweet, oozing golden,
thirsting for a girl's rounded mouth,
but thirsting more for girlish,
ice-cold, snow-white, cutting
teeth: for these do
the hearts of all hot dates lust. Selah.

Like, all too like
that aforesaid southern fruit
do I lie here, by little
flying insects
danced and played around,
and by even smaller,
more foolish and more wicked
desires and notions –
besieged by you,
you silent girl-kittens
full of misgivings,
Dudu and Suleika
– *sphinxed round*, that I may cram
much feeling into two words:

(– vergebe mir Gott
diese Sprachsünde! . . .)
– sitze hier, die beste Luft schnüffelnd,
Paradieses-Luft wahrlich,
lichte leichte Luft, goldgestreifte,
so gute Luft nur je
vom Monde herabfiel,
sei es aus Zufall
oder geschah es aus Übermute?
wie die alten Dichter erzählen.
Ich Zweifler aber ziehe es in Zweifel,
dafür komme ich
aus Europa,
das zweifelsüchtiger ist als alle Eheweibchen.
Möge Gott es bessern!
Amen.

Diese schönste Luft atmend,
mit Nüstern geschwellt gleich Bechern,
ohne Zukunft, ohne Erinnerungen,
so sitze ich hier, ihr
allerliebsten Freundinnen,
und sehe der Palme zu,
wie sie, einer Tänzerin gleich,
sich biegt, und schmiegt und in der Hüfte wiegt
– man tut es mit, sieht man lange zu . . .
einer Tänzerin gleich, die, wie mir scheinen will,
zu lange schon, gefährlich lange
immer, immer nur auf *einem* Beinchen stand?
– da vergaß sie darob, wie mir scheinen will,
das *andre* Beinchen?
Vergebens wenigstens
suchte ich das vermißte
Zwillings-Kleinod

(– may God forgive me
this sin of speech! . . .)
– I sit here sniffing the finest air,
air of Paradise, truly,
bright, buoyant air, gold-striped,
as good air as ever
fell from the moon –
came it by chance,
or did it happen by high spirits,
as the old poets tell?
I, however, call it
in question, since I come
from Europe,
which is more sceptical than any little wife.
May God improve it!
Amen.

Drinking in this finest air,
with nostrils swollen like goblets,
without future, without memories,
thus do I sit here, you
dearest maidens,
and regard the palm-tree,
and watch how, like a dancer,
it bends and bows and sways at the hips
– if you watch long you follow suit . . .
like a dancer who, it would seem,
has stood long, dangerously long,
always on *one* little leg?
– so that she has forgotten, it would seem,
the *other* leg?
At least, in vain
I sought the missing
twin-jewel

– nämlich das andre Beinchen –
in der heiligen Nähe
ihres allerliebsten, allerzierlichsten
Fächer- und Flatter- und Flitter-Röckchens.
Ja, wenn ihr mir, ihr schönen Freundinnen,
ganz glauben wollt:
sie hat es *verloren* . . .
Hu! Hu! Hu! Hu! Huh! . . .
Es ist dahin,
auf ewig dahin,
das andre Beinchen!
O schade um dies liebliche andre Beinchen!
Wo – mag es wohl weilen und verlassen trauern,
dieses einsame Beinchen?
In Furcht vielleicht vor einem
grimmen gelben blondgelockten
Löwen-Untiere? oder gar schon
abgenagt, abgeknappert –
erbärmlich! wehe! wehe! abgeknabbert! Sela.

O weint mir nicht,
weiche Herzen!
Weint mir nicht, ihr
Dattel-Herzen! Milch-Busen!
Ihr Süßholz-Herz-
Beutelchen!
Sei ein Mann, Suleika! Mut! Mut!

Weine nicht mehr,
bleiche Dudu!
– Oder sollte vielleicht
etwas Stärkeres, Herz-Stärkendes
hier am Platze sein?

– that is, the other leg –
in the sacred vicinity
of her dearest, daintiestfluttering, flickering, fan-
swirling little skirt.
Yes, if you would quite believe me,
you sweet maidens:
she has *lost* it . . .
Oh dear! oh dear! oh dear! oh dear! oh dear!
It has gone,
gone for ever,
the other leg!
Oh, what a shame about that other dear leg!
Where – can it be now, sorrowing and forsaken,
that lonely leg?
Perhaps in fear before an
angry, blond-maned
lion-monster? or perhaps even
gnawed off, broken in pieces –
pitiable, alas! alas! shattered in pieces! Selah.

Oh do not weep,
gentle hearts!
Do not weep, you
date-hearts! milk-bosoms!
You heart-caskets
of sweetwood!
Be a man, Suleika! Courage! Courage!

Weep no more,
pale Dudu!
– Or would perhaps
something more bracing, heart-bracing,
be in place here?

ein gesalbter Spruch?
ein feierlicher Zuspruch? . . .

Ha!
Herauf, Würde!
Blase, blase wieder,
Blasebalg der Tugend!
Ha!
Noch einmal brüllen,
moralisch brüllen,
als moralischer Löwe vor den Töchtern der Wüste brüllen!
– Denn Tugend-Geheul,
ihr allerliebsten Mädchen,
ist mehr als alles
Europäer-Inbrunst, Europäer-Heißhunger!
Und da stehe ich schon,
als Europäer,
ich kann nicht anders, Gott helfe mir!
Amen!

Die Wüste wächst: weh dem, der Wüsten birgt!
Stein knirscht an Stein, die Wüste schlingt und würgt.
Der ungeheure Tod blickt glühend braun
und *kaut* – , sein Leben ist sein Kaun . . .

Vergiß nicht, Mensch, den Wollust ausgeloht:
du – bist der Stein, die Wüste, bist der Tod . . .

an anointed proverb?
a solemn exhortation? . . .

Ha!
Up, dignity!
Blow, blow again,
bellows of virtue!
Ha!
Roar once again,
roar morally,
roar like a moral lion before the daughters of the desert!
– For virtuous howling,
you dearest maidens,
is loved best of all by
European ardour, European appetite!
And here I stand already,
as European
I cannot do otherwise, so help me God!
Amen!

The desert grows: woe to him who harbours deserts!
Stone grates on stone, the desert swallows down.
And death that *chews*, whose life is chewing,
gazes upon it, monstrous, glowing brown . . .

Consumed by lust, O Man, do not forget:
you – are the stone, the desert, you are death . . .

Letzter Wille

So sterben,
wie ich ihn einst sterben sah –,
den Freund, der Blitze und Blicke
göttlich in meine dunkle Jugend warf:
– mutwillig und tief,
in der Schlacht ein Tänzer –,

unter Kriegern der Heiterste,
unter Siegern der Schwerste,
auf seinem Schicksal ein Schicksal stehend,
hart, nachdenklich, vordenklich – :

erzitternd darob, *daß* er siegte,
jauchzend darüber, daß er *sterbend* siegte – :

befehlend, indem er starb,
– und er befahl, daß man *vernichte* . . .

So sterben,
wie ich ihn einst sterben sah:
siegend, *vernichtend* . . .

Last Will

So to die
as once I saw him die –
the friend who like a god
cast glances of lightning into my dark youth:
– wanton, profound,
in the slaughter a dancer –

of fighters the cheerfullest,
of victors the sternest,
a destiny standing upon his destiny,
firm, reflecting, preflecting – :

trembling with joy of victory,
rejoicing that he *died* in victory:

by dying, commanding
– and he commanded *destruction* . . .

So to die
as once I saw him die:
victorious, *destroying* . . .

Zwischen Raubvögeln

Wer hier hinab will,
wie schnell
schluckt den die Tiefe!
– Aber du, Zarathustra,
liebst den Abgrund noch,
tust der *Tanne* es gleich? –

Die schlägt Wurzeln, wo
der Fels selbst schaudernd
zur Tiefe blickt – ,
die zögert an Abgründen,
wo alles rings
hinunter will:
zwischen der Ungeduld
wilden Gerölls, stürzenden Bachs
geduldig duldend, hart, schweigsam,
einsam . . .

Einsam!
Wer wagte es auch,
hier zu Gast zu sein,
dir Gast zu sein? . . .
Ein Raubvogel vielleicht,
der hängt sich wohl
dem standhaften Dulder
schadenfroh ins Haar,
mit irrem Gelächter,
einem Raubvogel-Gelächter . . .

Wozu so standhaft?
– höhnt er grausam:

Amid Birds of Prey

He who descends here
how soon
the depths devour him!
– But you, Zarathustra,
you love the abyss,
as the *fir-tree* does? –

It strikes roots where
the cliff itself shudders
when it looks below –
it lingers at abysses
where everything
wants to plunge down:
amid the impatience
of savage rocks and precipitate streams
calmly forbearing, hard, silent,
solitary . . .

Solitary!
But who would dare
to visit here,
to visit *you*? . . .
A bird of prey perhaps,
he might hang,
with crazy laughter,
a bird of prey's laughter,
malicious, in the
patient stoic's hair . . .

Why so steadfast?
– he cruelly mocks:

man muß Flügel haben, wenn man den Abgrund liebt . . .
man muß nicht hängen bleiben,
wie du, Gehängter! –

O Zarathustra,
grausamster Nimrod!
Jüngst Jäger noch Gottes,
das Fangnetz aller Tugend,
der Pfeil des Bösen! –
Jetzt –
von dir selber erjagt,
deine eigene Beute,
in dich selber eingebohrt . . .

Jetzt –
einsam mit dir,
zwiesam im eignen Wissen,
zwischen hundert Spiegeln
vor dir selber falsch,
zwischen hundert Erinnerungen
ungewiß,
an jeder Wunde müd,
an jedem Froste kalt,
in eignen Stricken gewürgt,
Selbstkenner!
Selbsthenker!

Was bandest du dich
mit dem Strick deiner Weisheit?
Was locktest du dich
ins Paradies der alten Schlange?
Was schlichst du dich ein
in *dich* – in *dich*? . . .

if you love abysses you must have wings . . .
and not just hang there,
as you do, hanged man! –

O Zarathustra,
cruellest Nimrod!
Lately God's huntsman,
net to net all virtue,
arrow of the wicked! –
Now –
hunted down by yourself,
your own booty,
burrowed into yourself . . .

Now –
alone with yourself,
twofold in self-knowledge,
amid a hundred mirrors
false before yourself,
amid a hundred memories
uncertain,
wearied by every wound,
frozen by every frost,
choked in your own net,
self-knower!
self-hangman!

Why did you trap
yourself in your wisdom?
Why did you lure yourself
into the old serpent's garden?
why did you creep
into *yourself* – into *yourself?* . . .

Ein Kranker nun,
der an Schlangengift krank ist;
ein Gefangner nun,
der das härteste Los zog:
im eignen Schachte
gebückt arbeitend,
in dich selber eingehöhlt,
dich selber angrabend,
unbehilflich,
steif,
ein Leichnam – ,
von hundert Lasten übertürmt,
von dir überlastet,
ein *Wissender!*
ein *Selbsterkenner!*
der *weise* Zarathustra! . . .

Du suchtest die schwerste Last:
da fandest du *dich* – ,
du wirfst dich nicht ab von dir . . .

Lauernd,
kauernd,
einer, der schon nicht mehr aufrecht steht!
Du verwächst mir noch mit deinem Grabe,
verwachsener Geist! . . .

Und jüngst noch so stolz,
auf allen Stelzen deines Stolzes!
Jüngst noch der Einsiedler ohne Gott,
der Zweisiedler mit dem Teufel,
der scharlachne Prinz jedes Übermuts! . . .

Sick now
of the serpent's poison;
a prisoner now
with the hardest fate:
labouring bowed
in your own mine,
self-excavated,
digging into yourself,
awkward,
stiff,
a corpse –
overtowered by a hundred burdens,
overburdened with yourself,
a *man of knowledge*
who *knows himself!*
the *wise* Zarathustra! . . .

You sought the heaviest burden
and you found *yourself* –
it is a burden you cannot throw off . . .

Lying in wait,
crouching,
one who is no longer upright!
You shape yourself like your own grave,
misshapen spirit! . . .

And lately still so proud,
still on the stilts of your pride!
Lately still the godless hermit,
the dweller with the devil,
the high haughty scarlet prince! . . .

Jetzt –
zwischen zwei Nichtse
eingekrümmt,
ein Fragezeichen,
ein müdes Rätsel –
ein Rätsel für *Raubvögel* . . .
– sie werden dich schon "lösen",
sie hungern schon nach deiner "Lösung",
sie flattern schon um dich, ihr Rätsel,
um dich, Gehenkter! . . .
O Zarathustra! . . .
Selbstkenner! . . .
Selbsthenker! . . .

Now –
contorted
between two nothings,
a question-mark,
a weary riddle –
a riddle for *birds of prey* . . .
– they will soon "resolve" you,
already they thirst for your "resolution",
already they flutter about you, their riddle,
about you, hanged man! . . .
O Zarathustra! . . .
Self-knower! . . .
Self-hangman! . . .

Das Feuerzeichen

Hier, wo zwischen Meeren die Insel wuchs,
ein Opferstein jäh hinaufgetürmt,
hier zündet sich unter schwarzem Himmel
Zarathustra seine Höhenfeuer an, –
Feuerzeichen für verschlagne Schiffer,
Fragezeichen für solche, die Antwort haben . . .

Diese Flamme mit weißgrauem Bauche
– in kalte Fernen züngelt ihre Gier,
nach immer reineren Höhen biegt sie den Hals –
eine Schlange gerad aufgerichtet vor Ungeduld:
dieses Zeichen stellte ich vor mich hin.

Meine Seele selber ist diese Flamme:
unersättlich nach neuen Fernen
lodert aufwärts, aufwärts ihre stille Glut.
Was floh Zarathustra vor Tier und Menschen?
Was entlief er jäh allem festen Lande?
Sechs Einsamkeiten kennt er schon – ,
aber das Meer selbst war nicht genug ihm einsam,
die Insel ließ ihn steigen, auf dem Berg wurde er
    zur Flamme,
nach einer *siebenten* Einsamkeit
wirft er suchend jetzt die Angel über sein Haupt.

Verschlagne Schiffer! Trümmer alter Sterne!
Ihr Meere der Zukunft! Unausgeforschte Himmel!
nach allem Einsamen werfe ich jetzt die Angel:
gebt Antwort auf die Ungeduld der Flamme,
fangt mir, dem Fischer auf hohen Bergen,
meine siebente, *letzte* Einsamkeit! – –

The Fire-Signal

Here, where amid seas the island rose,
a steeply towering sacrificial stone,
here beneath a black sky Zarathustra
lit for himself his mountain fire –
a fire-signal for seamen blown off course,
a question-mark for those who possess answers . . .

This flame with light-grey belly
– its eager tongue flicking the chill horizon,
its neck arched out to ever purer heights –
a snake raised upright with impatience:
this signal I set up before me.

My soul, my soul itself, is this flame:
insatiable for new horizons
its silent glowing passion blazes upward.
Why did Zarathustra flee from beasts and men?
Why did he flee from all firm land?
Six solitudes he knew already –
but the sea itself had too little solitude for him,
the island welcomed him, and on the mountain he
    became a flame,
and when now he whirls his fishing-line
it is a *seventh* solitude he seeks to catch.

Seamen blown off course! Rubble of old stars!
You seas of the future! Unexplored sky!
to all that knows solitude do I now throw this line:
give answer to the flame's impatience,
catch me, the fisherman on high mountains,
my seventh, *final* solitude! – –

Die Sonne sinkt

I

Nicht lange durstest du noch,
     verbranntes Herz!
Verheißung ist in der Luft,
aus unbekannten Mündern bläst mich's an,
     – die große Kühle kommt . . .

Meine Sonne stand heiß über mir im Mittage:
seid mir gegrüßt, daß ihr kommt,
     ihr plötzlichen Winde,
ihr kühlen Geister des Nachmittags!

Die Luft geht fremd und rein.
Schielt nicht mit schiefem
     Verführerblick
die Nacht mich an? . . .
Bleib stark, mein tapfres Herz!
Frag nicht: warum?

The Sun Sinks

You shall not thirst much longer,
      scorched heart!
A promise is in the air,
from mouths unknown it wafts to me
      – great coolness comes . . .

My sun stood hot above me at midday:
welcome, sudden winds,
      now you have come,
cool spirits of the afternoon!

The air grows strange and clean.
Does night not look at me
      with sidelong
seductive eyes? . . .
Stay strong, brave heart!
Do not ask why. –

2

Tag meines Lebens!
die Sonne sinkt.
Schon steht die glatte
     Flut vergüldet.
Warm atmet der Fels:
     schlief wohl zu Mittag
das Glück auf ihm seinen Mittagsschlaf? –
     In grünen Lichtern
spielt Glück noch der braune Abgrund herauf.

Tag meines Lebens!
gen Abend gehts!
Schon glüht dein Auge
     halbgebrochen,
schon quillt deines Taus
     Tränengeträufel,
schon läuft still über weiße Meere
deiner Liebe Purpur,
deine letzte zögernde Seligkeit.

2

Day of my life!
the sun sinks.
Already the smooth
      flood stands gilded.
The cliffs breathe warmth:
      did happiness at midday
sleep there its midday sleep? –
      From the brown abyss
light and green it still dazzles up.

Day of my life!
it is almost evening!
Already the glow of your eye
      is half-dimmed,
already the tears of your dew
      are falling,
already there runs softly on the white sea
your love's purple,
your final hesitating bliss.

3

Heiterkeit, güldene, komm!
    du des Todes
heimlichster, süßester Vorgenuss!
– Lief ich zu rasch meines Wegs?
Jetzt erst, wo der Fuß müde ward,
    holt dein Blick mich noch ein,
    holt dein *Glück* mich noch ein.

Rings nur Welle und Spiel.
    Was je schwer war,
sank in blaue Vergessenheit –
müßig steht nun mein Kahn.
Sturm und Fahrt – wie verlernt er das!
    Wunsch und Hoffen ertrank,
    glatt liegt Seele und Meer.

Siebente Einsamkeit!
    Nie empfand ich
näher mir süße Sicherheit,
wärmer der Sonne Blick.
– Glüht nicht das Eis meiner Gipfel noch?
    Silbern, leicht, ein Fisch
    schwimmt nun mein Nachen hinaus . . .

3

Gilded cheerfulness, come!
      sweetest, secretest
foretaste of death!
– Did I run my course too quickly?
Only now, when my foot has grown weary,
      does your glance overtake me,
      does your *happiness* overtake me.

Only playing of waves all around.
      Whatever was hard
has sunk into blue oblivion –
my boat now lies idle.
Storm and voyaging – all forgotten now!
      Desire and hope have drowned,
      smooth lie soul and sea.

Seventh solitude!
      Never such sweet
security, never such
sunlight warmth.
– Does the ice of my summit still glow?
      Silver, light, a fish
      my little craft now swims out . . .

Klage der Ariadne

Wer wärmt mich, wer liebt mich noch?
      Gebt heiße Hände!
      gebt Herzens-Kohlenbecken!
Hingestreckt, schaudernd,
Halbtotem gleich, dem man die Füße wärmt,
geschüttelt ach! von unbekannten Fiebern,
zitternd vor spitzen eisigen Frostpfeilen,
      von dir gejagt, Gedanke!
Unnennbarer! Verhüllter, Entsetzlicher!
      Du Jäger hinter Wolken!
Darniedergeblitzt von dir,
du höhnisch Auge, das mich aus Dunklem anblickt!
      So liege ich,
biege mich, winde mich, gequält
von allen ewigen Martern,
      getroffen
von dir, grausamster Jäger,
du unbekannter – *Gott* . . .

Triff tiefer!
Triff einmal noch!
Zerstich, zerstich dies Herz!
Was soll dies Martern
mit zähnestumpfen Pfeilen?
Was blickst du wieder,
der Menschen-Qual nicht müde,
mit schadenfrohen Götter-Blitz-Augen?
Nicht töten willst du,
nur martern, martern?
Wozu – *mich* martern,
du schadenfroher unbekannter Gott?

Ariadne's Complaint

Who still warms me, who still loves me?
>Offer me hot hands!
>offer me coal-warmers for the heart!
Spread-eagled, shuddering,
like one half-dead whose feet are warmed –
shaken, alas! by unknown fevers,
trembling with sharp icy frost-arrows,
>pursued by you, my thought!
Unutterable, veiled, terrible one!
>Huntsman behind the clouds!
Struck down by your lightning-bolt,
you mocking eye that stares at me from the darkness!
>Thus I lie,
bend myself, twist myself, tortured
by every eternal torment,
>smitten
by you, cruel huntsman,
you unknown – *god* . . .

Strike deeper!
Strike once again!
Sting and sting, shatter this heart!
What means this torment
with blunt arrows?
Why do you look down,
unwearied of human pain,
with malicious divine flashing eyes?
Will you not kill,
only torment, torment?
Why – torment *me*,
you malicious, unknown god?

Haha!
du schleichst heran
bei solcher Mitternacht? . . .
Was willst du?
Sprich!
Du drängst mich, drückst mich,
Ha! schon viel zu nahe!
Du hörst mich atmen,
du behorchst mein Herz,
du Eifersüchtiger!
– worauf doch eifersüchtig?
Weg! Weg!
wozu die Leiter?
willst du *hinein,*
ins Herz, einsteigen,
in meine heimlichsten
Gedanken einsteigen?
Schamloser! Unbekannter! Dieb!
Was willst du dir erstehlen?
Was willst du dir erhorchen?
Was willst du dir erfoltern,
du Folterer
du – Henker-Gott!
Oder soll ich, dem Hunde gleich,
vor dir mich wälzen?
Hingebend, begeistert außer mir
dir Liebe – zuwedeln?

Umsonst!
Stich weiter!
Grausamster Stachel!
Kein Hund – dein Wild nur bin ich,
grausamster Jäger!
deine stolzeste Gefangne,

Ha ha!
Are you stealing near
at such a midnight hour? . . .
What do you want?
Speak!
You oppress me, press me,
Ha! far too closely!
You hear me breathing,
you overhear my heart,
you jealous god!
– yet jealous of what?
Away! Away!
Why the ladder?
Would you climb
into my heart,
climb into my
most secret thoughts?
Shameless, unknown thief!
What would you get by stealing?
What would you get by listening?
What would you get by torturing,
you torturer?
you – hangman-god!
Or shall I, like a dog,
roll before you?
Surrendering, raving with rapture,
wag – love to you?

In vain!
Strike again,
cruellest goad!
Not dog – I am only your game,
cruellest huntsman!
your proudest prisoner,

du Räuber hinter Wolken . . .
Sprich endlich!
Du Blitz-Verhüllter! Unbekannter! sprich!
Was willst du, Wegelagerer, von – *mir*? . . .

Wie?
Lösegeld?
Was willst du Lösegelds?
Verlange viel – das rät mein Stolz!
und rede kurz – das rät mein andrer Stolz!
Haha!
Mich – willst du? mich?
mich – ganz? . . .

Haha!
Und marterst mich, Narr, der du bist,
zermarterst meinen Stolz?
Gib *Liebe* mir – wer wärmt mich noch?
       wer liebt mich noch?
gib heiße Hände,
gib Herzens-Kohlenbecken,
gib mir, der Einsamsten,
die Eis, ach! siebenfaches Eis
nach Feinden selber,
nach Feinden schmachten lehrt,
gib, ja ergib,
grausamster Feind,
mir – *dich*! . . .
Davon!
Da floh er selber,
mein einziger Genoß,
mein großer Feind,
mein Unbekannter,
mein Henker-Gott! . . .

you robber behind the clouds . . .
For the last time, speak!
Veiled in lightning! Unknown! speak!
What do you want, waylayer, from – *me*?

What?
Ransom?
How much ransom?
Demand much – thus speaks my pride!
and be brief – thus speaks my other pride!
Ha! ha!
Me – you? want me?
me – all of me? . . .

Ha ha!
And you torment me, fool that you are,
you rack my pride?
Offer me *love* – who still warms me?
　　　who still loves me?
offer me hot hands,
offer me coal-warmers for the heart,
offer me, the most solitary,
whom ice, alas! sevenfold ice
has taught to long for enemies,
even for enemies,
offer, yes yield to me,
cruellest enemy –
yourself! . . .
He is gone!
He has fled,
my sole companion,
my great enemy,
my unknown,
my hangman-god! . . .

Nein!
komm zurück!
Mit allen deinen Martern!
All meine Tränen laufen
zu dir den Lauf
und meine letzte Herzensflamme
dir glüht sie auf.
O komm zurück,
mein unbekannter Gott! mein *Schmerz!*
    mein letztes Glück! . . .

Ein Blitz. Dionysos wird in smaragdener Schönheit sichtbar.

DIONYSOS:
Sei klug, Ariadne! . . .
Du hast kleine Ohren, du hast meine Ohren:
steck ein kluges Wort hinein! –
Muß man sich nicht erst hassen, wenn man sich lieben
    soll? . . .

Ich bin dein Labyrinth . . .

No!
come back!
with all your torments!
All the streams of my tears
run their course to you!
and the last flame of my heart,
it burns up to you.
Oh come back,
my unknown god! my *pain!*
     my last happiness! . . .

A flash of lightning. Dionysus becomes visible in emerald beauty.

  DIONYSUS:
Be wise, Ariadne! . . .
You have little ears, you have ears like mine:
let some wisdom into them! –
Must we not first hate ourself if we are to love
    ourself? . . .

I am thy labyrinth . . .

Ruhm und Ewigkeit

1

Wie lange sitzest du schon
    auf deinem Mißgeschick?
Gib acht! du brütest mir noch
    ein Ei,
    ein Basilisken-Ei
aus deinem langen Jammer aus.

Was schleicht Zarathustra entlang dem Berge? –

Mißtrauisch, geschwürig, düster,
ein langer Lauerer – ,
aber plötzlich, ein Blitz,
hell, furchtbar, ein Schlag
gen Himmel aus dem Abgrund:
– dem Berge selber schüttelt sich
das Eingeweide . . .

Wo Haß und Blitzstrahl
Eins ward, ein *Fluch* – ,
auf den Bergen haust jetzt Zarathustras Zorn,
eine Wetterwolke schleicht er seines Wegs.

Verkrieche sich, wer eine letzte Decke hat!
Ins Bett mit euch, ihr Zärtlinge!
Nun rollen Donner über die Gewölbe,
nun zittert, was Gebälk und Mauer ist,
nun zucken Blitze und schwefelgelbe Wahrheiten –
    Zarathustra *flucht* . . .

Fame and Eternity

I

How long have you already brooded
        upon your misfortune?
Take care! you will yet hatch
        an egg,
        a basilisk egg,
out of your protracted misery.

Why does Zarathustra slink along beside the mountain? –

Mistrustful, ulcerous, gloomy,
long lying in wait –
then suddenly, a lightning-flash,
bright, fearful, a blow
towards the sky from the abyss:
– the mountain itself feels
its intestines shake . . .

Where hate and lightning
became one, a *curse* –
on the mountains Zarathustra's wrath now makes its
        home,
slinks along its path a thundercloud.

Whoever has a shelter, let him seek it!
Away with you to bed, you weaklings!
Now thunders roll over the vaulted roofs,
now trembles what is wall and timber-work,
now lightnings flash and brimstone-coloured truths –
        Zarathustra *curses* . . .

2

Diese Münze, mit der
alle Welt bezahlt,
Ruhm – ,
mit Handschuhen fasse ich diese Münze an,
mit Ekel trete ich sie *unter* mich.

Wer will bezahlt sein?
Die Käuflichen . . .
Wer *feil* steht, greift
mit fetten Händen
nach diesem Allerwelts-Blechklingklang Ruhm!

– *Willst* du sie kaufen?
Sie sind alle käuflich.
Aber biete viel!
klingle mit vollem Beutel!
– du *stärkst* sie sonst,
du stärkst sonst ihre *Tugend* . . .

Sie sind alle tugendhaft.
Ruhm und Tugend – das reimt sich.
So lange die Welt lebt,
zahlt sie Tugend-Geplapper
mit Ruhm-Geklapper – ,
die Welt *lebt* von diesem Lärm . . .

Vor allen Tugendhaften
        will ich schuldig sein,
schuldig heißen mit jeder großen Schuld!
Vor allen Ruhms-Schalltrichtern
wird mein Ehrgeiz zum Wurm – ,
unter solchen gelüstets mich,
der *Niedrigste* zu sein . . .

2

This coin with which
all the world makes payment,
fame –
I grasp this coin with gloves,
with loathing I trample it *beneath* me.

Who wants to be paid?
The buyable . . .
He who is *for sale*
reaches with greasy hands
for this everybodys-jingling-tinpot fame!

– Do you *want* to buy them?
They are all buyable.
But offer much!
jingle a full purse!
– or you will *fortify* them,
you will fortify their *virtue* . . .

They are all virtuous.
Fame and virtue – they go together.
For as long as the world lives
it pays chatter of virtue
with clatter of fame –
the world *lives* by this racket . . .

To all the virtuous
        I want to be in debt,
of every great offence called guilty!
Before all bell-mouths of fame
my ambition becomes a worm –
of such I desire to be
the *lowest* . . .

Diese Münze, mit der
alle Welt bezahlt,
Ruhm – ,
mit Handschuhen fasse ich diese Münze an,
mit Ekel trete ich sie *unter* mich.

3

Still! –
Von großen Dingen – ich *sehe* Großes! –
soll man schweigen
oder groß reden:
rede groß, meine entzückte Weisheit!

Ich sehe hinauf –
dort rollen Lichtmeere:
o Nacht, o Schweigen, o totenstiller Lärm! . . .
Ich sehe ein Zeichen – ,
aus fernsten Fernen
sinkt langsam funkelnd ein Sternbild gegen mich . . .

4

Höchstes Gestirn des Seins!
Ewiger Bildwerke Tafel!
Du kommst zu mir? –
Was keiner erschaut hat,
deine stumme Schönheit –
wie? sie flieht vor meinen Blicken nicht? –

Schild der Notwendigkeit!
Ewiger Bildwerke Tafel!
– aber du weißt es ja:

This coin with which
all the world makes payment,
fame –
I grasp this coin with gloves,
with loathing I trample it *beneath* me.

3

Soft! –
Of great things – I *see* something great! –
one should keep silent
or speak greatly:
speak greatly, my enraptured wisdom!

I look above me –
there seas of light are rolling:
oh night, oh silence, oh deathly silent uproar! . . .
I see a sign –
from the farthest distance
slowly glittering a constellation sinks towards me . . .

4

Highest star of being!
Eternal tablet of forms!
You come to me? –
What none has beheld,
your speechless beauty –
what? it flees not from my gaze? –

Image of what must be!
Eternal tablet of forms!
– but you know it:

was alle hassen,
was allein *ich* liebe:
– daß *du ewig* bist!
daß du *notwendig* bist! –
meine Liebe entzündet
sich ewig nur an der Notwendigkeit.

Schild der Notwendigkeit!
Höchstes Gestirn des Seins!
– das kein Wunsch erreicht,
– das kein Nein befleckt,
ewiges Ja des Seins,
ewig bin ich dein Ja:
denn ich liebe dich, o Ewigkeit! – –

what everyone else hates,
what *I* alone love:
– that *you* are *eternal!*
that you *must be!* –
my love is ignited
only by that which must be.

Image of what must be!
Highest star of being!
– what no longing attains,
– no denial defiles,
eternal Yes of being,
eternally am I thy Yes:
for I love thee, O eternity! – –

Von der Armut des Reichsten

Zehn Jahre dahin – ,
kein Tropfen erreichte mich,
kein feuchter Wind, kein Tau der Liebe
– ein *regenloses* Land . . .
Nun bitte ich meine Weisheit,
nicht geizig zu werden in dieser Dürre:
ströme selber über, träufle selber Tau,
sei selber Regen der vergilbten Wildnis!

Einst hieß ich die Wolken
fortgehn von meinen Bergen, –
einst sprach ich "mehr Licht, ihr Dunklen!"
Heut locke ich sie, daß sie kommen:
macht Dunkel um mich mit euren Eutern!
– ich will euch melken,
ihr Kühe der Höhe!
Milchwarme Weisheit, süßen Tau der Liebe
ströme ich über das Land.

Fort, fort, ihr Wahrheiten,
die ihr düster blickt!
Nicht will ich auf meinen Bergen
herbe ungeduldige Wahrheiten sehn.
Vom Lächeln vergüldet
nahe mir heut die Wahrheit,
von der Sonne gesüßt, von der Liebe gebräunt, –
eine *reife* Wahrheit breche ich allein vom Baum.

Heut strecke ich die Hand aus
nach den Locken des Zufalls,

Of the Poverty of the Richest Man

Ten years have passed –
no drop of water has reached me,
no moist wind, no dew of love
– a *rainless* land . . .
Now I ask of my wisdom
that it grow not mean in this aridity:
yourself overflow, yourself drop dew,
yourself be rain to this yellowed wilderness!

Once I bade the clouds
depart my mountains –
once I said "more light, dark clouds!"
Today I lure them to come back:
make darkness round me with your udders!
– I want to milk you,
cows of the heights!
Milkwarm wisdom, secret dew of love
I pour down over the land.

Be gone, be gone, truths
of gloomy aspect!
I want on my mountain
no acid fretful truths.
Golden with smiles
let truth approach me today,
made sweet by the sun, made brown by love,
ripe truths alone do I pluck from the vine.

Today I stretched out my hand
to the hairy head of chance,

klug genug, den Zufall
einem Kinde gleich zu führen, zu überlisten.
Heut will ich gastfreundlich sein
gegen Unwillkommnes,
gegen das Schicksal selbst will ich nicht stachlicht sein,
– Zarathustra ist kein Igel.

Meine Seele,
unersättlich mit ihrer Zunge,
an alle guten und schlimmen Dinge hat sie schon geleckt,
in jede Tiefe tauchte sie hinab.
Aber immer gleich dem Korke,
immer schwimmt sie wieder obenauf,
sie gaukelt wie Öl über braune Meere:
dieser Seele halber heißt man mich den Glücklichen.

Wer sind mir Vater und Mutter?
Ist nicht mir Vater Prinz Überfluß
und Mutter das stille Lachen?
Erzeugte nicht dieser beiden Ehebund
mich Rätseltier,
mich Lichtunhold,
mich Verschwender aller Weisheit, Zarathustra?

Krank heute vor Zärtlichkeit,
ein Tauwind,
sitzt Zarathustra wartend, wartend auf seinen Bergen, –
im eignen Safte
süß geworden und gekocht,
unterhalb seines Gipfels,
unterhalb seines Eises,
müde und selig,
ein Schaffender an seinem siebenten Tag.

cunning enough to outwit chance
and lead it along like a child.
Today I will be hospitable
to things unwelcome,
towards fate itself I will not be prickly
– Zarathustra is no hedgehog.

My soul,
its tongue insatiable,
has licked at every good and evil thing,
dived down into every depth.
But always, like a cork,
always it comes bobbing up again,
it juggles like oil on the brown surface of the sea:
on account of this my soul they call me: the happy man.

Who are my father and mother?
Is my father not Prince Abundance
and my mother a silent laughter?
Did the marriage of this couple not engender
this enigmatic beast,
this demon of light,
this squanderer of wisdom, Zarathustra?

Sick today with tenderness,
a thawing wind,
Zarathustra sits waiting, waiting in his mountains –
in his own juice
cooked and grown sweet,
below his summit,
below his ice,
tired and happy,
a creator on his seventh day.

– Still!
Eine Wahrheit wandelt über mir
einer Wolke gleich, –
mit unsichtbaren Blitzen trifft sie mich.
Auf breiten langsamen Treppen
steigt ihr Glück zu mir:
komm, komm, geliebte Wahrheit!

– Still!
Meine Wahrheit ists! –
Aus zögernden Augen,
aus samtenen Schaudern
trifft mich ihr Blick,
lieblich, bös, ein Mädchenblick . . .
Sie erriet meines Glückes *Grund*,
sie erriet *mich* – ha! was sinnt sie aus? –
Purpurn lauert ein Drache
im Abgrunde ihres Mädchenblicks.

– Still! Meine Wahreit *redet!* –

Wehe dir, Zarathustra!

Du siehst aus, wie einer,
der Gold verschluckt hat:
man wird dir noch den Bauch aufschlitzen! . . .

Zu reich bist du,
du Verderber vieler!
Zu viele machst *du* neidisch,
zu viele machst du arm . . .
Mir selber wirft dein Licht Schatten – ,

– Soft!
A truth passes over me
like a cloud –
strikes me with invisible lightnings.
On broad slow stairways
its happiness climbs up to me:
come, come, beloved truth!

– Soft!
It is *my* truth! –
From hesitant eyes,
from velvet tremblings
its glance strikes at me,
lovely, wicked, the glance of a girl . . .
She divines the *ground* of my happiness,
she divines *me* – ha! what is she thinking of? –
Purple there lurks a dragon
in the abyss of her glance.

– Soft! My truth *speaks!* –

Woe to thee, Zarathustra!

You resemble one
who has swallowed gold:
you will yet have your belly cut open! . . .

You are too rich,
corrupter of many!
You make too many envious,
you make too many poor . . .
Even I am cast in shadow by your light –

es fröstelt mich: geh weg, du Reicher,
geh, Zarathustra, weg aus deiner Sonne! . . .

Du möchtest schenken, wegschenken deinen Überfluß,
aber du selber bist der Überflüssigste!
Sei klug, du Reicher!
Verschenke dich selber erst, o Zarathustra!

Zehn Jahre dahin – ,
und kein Tropfen erreichte dich?
kein feuchter Wind? kein Tau der Liebe?
Aber wer *sollte* dich auch lieben,
du Überreicher?
Dein Glück macht rings trocken,
macht arm an Liebe
– ein *regenloses* Land . . .

Neimand dankt dir mehr.
Du aber dankst jedem,
der von dir nimmt:
daran erkenne ich dich,
du Überreicher,
du *Ärmster* aller Reichen!

Du opferst dich, dich *quält* dein Reichtum – ,
du gibst dich ab,
du schonst dich nicht, du liebst dich nicht:
die große Qual zwingt dich allezeit,
die Qual *übervoller* Scheuern, *übervollen* Herzens –
aber niemand dankt dir mehr . . .

Du mußt *ärmer* werden,
weiser Unweiser!
willst du geliebt sein.

I grow cold: away, man gifted with riches,
away, Zarathustra, out of your sunlight! . . .

You would like to bestow, to give away your superfluity,
but you yourself are the most superfluous!
Be sensible, man gifted with riches!
First give yourself, O Zarathustra!

Ten years have passed –
and no drop of water has reached you?
no moist wind? no dew of love?
But who *could* love you,
man superabundant in riches?
Your happiness makes all around you arid,
makes it poor in love
– a *rainless* land . . .

No one thanks you now.
But you thank everyone
who takes from you:
that is how I know you,
superabundant in riches,
poorest of all the rich!

You offer yourself, your riches *torment* you –
you deliver yourself up,
you do not spare yourself, do not love yourself:
the great torment constrains you always,
the torment of barns *overfull*, of a heart *overfull* –
but no one thanks you now . . .

You must grow *poorer*,
unwise man of wisdom!
if you want to be loved.

Man liebt nur die Leidenden,
man gibt Liebe nur dem Hungernden:
verschenke dich selbst erst, o Zarathustra!

– Ich bin deine Wahrheit . .

Only the suffering are loved,
love is given only to the hungry man:
first give yourself, O Zarathustra!

– I am thy truth . . .

AWARENESS NOT ONLY HELPS YOU
ACCEPT AND LOVE YOUR FATE
AMOR FATI

BUT ALSO, AWARENESS
THAT ONE BECOMES
WHAT ONE PRACTICES

CAN SERVE AS A MOTIVE
IN ITSELF

※ Like Nietzsche I am too
powerful to waste time unpicking the
knots left by other philosophers I burst
through them
with a nod
only.

★ Nietzsche never
really understood
the inevitable part
of the Global will to Power
that benefits from
contracts, social binding
constraints
Sync, channel, grew
in other words, Apollo.

He was to human focussed/
centred

We need both
but in proportion.

Notes

The following notes are mainly biographical and seek to place the poems in the context of Nietzsche's life and works.

Only a Fool! Only a Poet! (page 23)

This opening poem was first printed, in a slightly different version, in the fourth part of *Thus Spoke Zarathustra* (1885), where it is included in the chapter called "The Song of Melancholy" and put into the mouth of "the old sorcerer". The action of *Zarathustra* Part Four involves the appearance in Zarathustra's remote mountainous territory of a number of "higher men" whose specific errors and shortcomings are revealed to them during their brief sojourn there. Among them is "the old sorcerer", and it is universally agreed that he is Richard Wagner and thus, by an extension very amply documented in Nietzsche's other writings, the epitome of "the artist". Now, for reasons which should become clear when we come to discuss the following poem, I would contend that the three *Dithyrambs of Dionysus* included in the fourth part of *Zarathustra* were inserted there capriciously and by force – that is, that they were originally composed independently of *Zarathustra* and do not truly belong in that book. In this present instance, however, little argumentation is called for: if, as seems to be obviously the case, "Zarathustra" is Nietzsche's ideal self, the "higher men" are, as well as being other identifiable individuals or types, also facets of Nietzsche's own character of which he at least in part disapproves, repudiates and, in the visionary conclusion of *Thus Spoke Zarathustra*, overcomes; the one represented by the sorcerer, Wagner, is Nietzsche as artist, and in this poem specifically as poet, and the poem thus rightly belongs at the head of the present collection of poems. In the chapter of *Zarathustra* called "Of Poets", Zarathustra is asked why he once said that the poets lie too much: he replies: "What did Zarathustra once say to you? That the poets lie too much?

– But Zarathustra too is a poet. Do you now believe that he spoke the truth? Why do you believe it?" Granted, however, he goes on, that "someone has said in all seriousness that the poets lie too much: he is right – *we* do lie too much. We know too little and are bad learners: so we have to lie."

The Desert Grows: Woe to Him Who Harbours Deserts . . . (page 31)

This poem too was inserted, in a form only slightly different from that in which it appears here, in Part Four of *Thus Spoke Zarathustra*. There it is placed in the mouth of "the wanderer who called himself Zarathustra's shadow" and who is usually regarded as representing the "freethinker". It constitutes the greater part of the chapter called "Among the Daughters of the Desert". The "higher men" have just been treated by Zarathustra to a banquet and the sorcerer has, by way of post-prandial entertainment, spoiled the prevailing spirit of gaiety with a recital of "Only a fool! Only a poet!" It is in response to this, and with the intention of restoring his fellow guests' good humour, that the shadow sings them his poem "The desert grows". – "I have seen many lands", he says in preamble,

> my nose has learned to test and appraise many kinds of air: but with you my nostrils taste their greatest delight! Except, except – oh forgive an old memory! Forgive me an old after-dinner song that I once composed among the daughters of the desert – for with them there was the same good, clear oriental air; there I was furthest away from cloudy, damp, melancholy Old Europe! In those days I loved such oriental girls and other blue kingdoms of heaven, over which no clouds and no thoughts hung. You would not believe how prettily they sat there when they were not dancing, deep but without thoughts, like little secrets, like ribboned riddles, like after-dinner nuts – motley and strange indeed! but without clouds: riddles that one can read: to please such girls I then devised an after-dinner psalm.

Whereupon he sings his song "with a kind of roaring". Now even in the context of the fourth part of *Zarathustra*, whose action is so structured that almost anything could take place, this poem seems an irrelevance and a capricious insert: even more obviously than "Only a Fool! Only a Poet!" it originates outside the Zarathustra-world and is a piece of pure autobiography. H.W. Brann was, so far as I know, the first to assert in print that it is a lightly disguised recollection of a visit to a brothel (in *Nietzsche und die Frauen*, 1931). The evidence for this assertion seems to me compelling and the interpretation plainly correct. The poem itself, with its setting and near *doubles entendres*, can easily be interpreted in this sense without strain and regardless of who wrote it: so nearly unequivocal is it, indeed, that one would almost have to prove that this interpretation was *not* correct. Knowing it is by Nietzsche, however, we can also draw on evidence extraneous to it. In the most general sense it can be said that, since he was a student at two German universities in the 1860s and 1870s, it would not be in any way unusual if he had visited a brothel, at any rate once: it was a normal student practice. And it happens that we have an account, almost certainly in his own words, of an occasion when he was taken to one. It is contained in the recollections of a fellow student, the philologist Paul Deussen, published in 1901. In February 1865 both were students at Bonn, and Nietzsche told him, Deussen says, that he had paid a visit to Cologne, where a cab driver had driven him around and when he finally asked to be taken to a good restaurant the driver had transported him to a brothel instead. "I suddenly saw myself surrounded by half-a-dozen apparitions in tinsel and gauze, who looked at me expectantly", Nietzsche told him. "I stood for a moment speechless. Then I made for a piano in the room as to the only living thing in that company and struck several chords. They broke the spell and I hurried away." This brief passage in Deussen's *Erinnerungen an Friedrich Nietzsche* has created a small literature of its own, culminating in Thomas Mann's *Doctor Faustus*, since it is the only concrete piece of evidence we have which links Nietzsche's mental and physical breakdown with what must almost certainly have been its cause.

There can be very little doubt by now, when every aspect and almost every week of Nietzsche's life have been scrutinized from every possible angle, that the illness he suffered from was syphilis (which in his day was incurable) or that, in the total absence of any evidence to the contrary, he contracted it from a prostitute. It has been shown that he was treated for a syphilitic infection by two doctors in Leipzig during 1867; and there is much in his singular and tragic existence that is explicable only by supposing he knew, or strongly suspected, what his "illness" actually was (though almost certainly he failed to realize what the full extent of its consequences would be).

Last Will (page 41)

This is probably the earliest of the *Dithyrambs of Dionysus*: it appears in a notebook of 1883 which also contains notes for Part Three of *Zarathustra*. I am unable to say who the dying man is, or even to suggest a candidate: notwithstanding that 1883 is the year of Wagner's death, it is certainly not him. Possibly the figure is imaginary; for there seem to be clear links between "Last Will" and one of the best-known chapters of *Zarathustra*, "Of Voluntary Death", the burden of which is that one should "die at the right time" so that one's death will be "a spur and a promise to the living".

Amid Birds of Prey (page 43)

At first entitled "Am Abgrunde" ("At the Abyss"), "Zwischen Raubvögeln" is the harshest of Nietzsche's many hymns to solitude. One of the soundest reasons for identifying Nietzsche with Zarathustra – a procedure which might otherwise seem simplistic – is the extremity of the solitude into which Zarathustra is driven: patently a heroic projection of Nietzsche's own lonely status. It is hard to think of anyone who in the middle of modern Europe succeeded in segregating himself from almost every kind of attachment so completely as Nietzsche did. That at bottom he chose and preferred isolation is, of course, obvious; and that he should have made a heroic virtue of this choice was, given his love of self-dramatization, almost inevitable: but that does not mean that he did not suffer as a result of it. So it is that we find, throughout his works, together with celebrations of self-sufficiency, reflections on the perils attending it: the chief of these appears to be that the opportunity afforded for self-absorption will lead to an increase in self-knowledge and -awareness so great as to be self-destructive. This is the "abyss" over which Zarathustra "hangs" in his mountain redoubt. This poem too is, like the preceding poems, autobiography; it is the final stage of a quasi-dramatic development. The last chapter of *Human, All Too Human* is called "Man Alone with Himself"; in *Zarathustra* Nietzsche drew a full-length portrait of a man alone with himself; now, at the end of his course, the man alone with himself discovers that, through his self-imposed solitude, he has become his own executioner.

The Fire-Signal (page 51)

These twenty-seven measured, solemn and impressive lines employ the vocabulary and setting of *Thus Spoke Zarathustra* but go one step beyond it. Perhaps we are permitted to recognize in the "six solitudes" which Zarathustra already knows an allusion to his condition at the conclusion of the book named after him: if so, the "seventh solitude" he seeks would represent a new and final stage in his spiritual journey. That this "seventh solitude" is intended to be taken in a fairly literal sense as a description of the years immediately preceding the collecting together of the *Dithyrambs of Dionysus* can, I believe, be shown from the persistence in Nietzsche's mind, after the other Zarathustra-metaphors had been left behind, of the metaphor of "fishing for men" which *Thus Spoke Zarathustra* shares with the New Testament. Like the disciples of Jesus, Zarathustra too was a "fisher of men" who differed from the fishermen of religion chiefly in the kind of bait he used; now, however, he has commenced fishing in a place where even the most enticing bait will catch nothing, namely "on high mountains": thus he explains to himself the absence of any catch except a "seventh solitude". This state of things corresponds precisely to the actual state of things in Nietzsche's life at the time the poem was probably written: though convinced of the tremendous importance to mankind of what he had to tell them, he completely lacked an audience; and he acquired one only after his mental breakdown. "To all that was tragic in Nietzsche's life", George Brandes wrote in 1900 in his obituary of him, "was added this: that, after thirsting for recognition to the point of morbidity, he attained it in an altogether fantastic degree when, though still living, he was shut out from life." Nietzsche himself continued to the end to account for his isolation by employing the fishing metaphor. Writing in *Ecce Homo* of *Beyond Good and Evil*, the book which succeeded *Zarathustra*, he says:

> The task for the immediately following years was as clear as it could be. Now that the affirmative part of my task was done, it was the turn of the denying, the No-saying and No-*doing* part: the revaluation of existing values themselves, the great war – the evocation of a day of decision. Included here is the slow search for those related to me, for such as out of strength would offer me their hand for *the work of destruction*. – From now on all my writings are fish-hooks: perhaps I understand fishing as well as anyone? . . . If nothing got *caught* I am not to blame. *There were no fish.*

Though the connection is not absolutely direct, I believe this passage and "The Fire-Signal" to be parallel statements of the same thing.

The Sun Sinks (page 53)

The sense of the sixth and by far the calmest of the *Dithyrambs of Dionysus* is unambiguous to a degree rare in Nietzsche's visionary poems. It is a description of his own death – or, more precisely, of what he anticipates, or at least hopes, his death will be like. What is extremely striking about the poem is the degree to which its imagery is drawn from the stock of simple images and metaphors which Nietzsche has already employed time and again to express feelings of happiness and contentment:

their repetition here produces, for anyone who knows Nietzsche's poetic works as a whole, a coda-like effect. Mostly their meaning is so obvious as to make any elucidation superfluous, though it might be worthwhile to draw attention to the number of colours named: gold ("gilt"), green, brown, white, purple, blue, silver. To speak of a "colour symbolism" in Nietzsche's poetry and poetic prose would be to speak too solemnly; but certain colours did have a special significance for him and mention of them is intended to constitute something more than natural description. Gold is, as in the present poem, the colour of the sea when the setting sun is level with it, and it is thus the colour of late evening and of the moods appropriate to that time of day. Brown – which from the number of times he employs it might almost be called Nietzsche's favourite colour – is the colour of wine-grapes when they are perfectly ripe and ready to be harvested, and is thus the colour of sweetness and maturity.

Ariadne's Complaint (page 59)

The seventh of the *Dithyrambs of Dionysus* has a very strange history. It first appeared, without its title and dramatized ending, in Part Four of *Zarathustra*, in the chapter called "The Sorcerer". As already remarked, the sorcerer is Richard Wagner, and when Zarathustra first encounters him he is "throwing his arms about as if in a frenzy"; at length he hurls himself to the ground, and when Zarathustra approaches him he is revealed to be "a trembling old man with staring eyes". Failing to realize he is no longer alone, the sorcerer "continually looked around him with pathetic gestures. . . . Eventually, however, after much trembling, quivering and self-contortion, he began to wail thus" – and then follows "Who still warms me, who still loves me?" But the song has so ill an effect on Zarathustra that before the sorcerer has finished "he could restrain himself no longer; he took his stick and struck the wailing man with all his force. 'Stop!' he shouted at him with furious laughter. 'Stop, you actor! You fabricator! You liar from the heart! I know you well! . . .'" The grotesque and unpleasing scene continues on for some time, with the sorcerer acquiring increasing enlightenment as to his true nature from the all-knowing Zarathustra. It must therefore disconcert us to hear the sorcerer's "lying" lament now proceeding from the semi-divine Ariadne and addressed to the wholly divine Diony-sus under circumstances which make it impossible to think that the sentiments it expresses are not intended to be taken in earnest. Some explanation is obviously called for, yet there is none that is satisfactory on the "objective", artistic level, and one might be inclined to call this reemployment of the poem in a quite different context an artistic blunder. In the last resort, I believe, this judgement must prevail: the two contexts, both dramatic, in which the poem is employed are artistically irreconcilable with one another, and the poem itself is thus irresolvably ambiguous. On the biographical level, however, the scene in *Zarathustra* and the scene on Naxos are intimately connected, and it is in this connection that we must seek the cause of the artistic error.

In September or October 1887, while staying in Venice, the city Wagner died in, Nietzsche set down the following brief notes for a dramatic sketch:

Satyr play at the end
Insert: brief conversation between Dionysus, Theseus and Ariadne
– Theseus is becoming absurd, said Ariadne, Theseus is becoming virtuous – Theseus jealous of Ariadne's dream. Ariadne's complaint. The hero admiring himself, becoming absurd.
Dionysus without jealousy: "That which I love in you, how could a Theseus love that" – – – Last act. Wedding of Diony-sus and Ariadne.
"One is not jealous when one is a god", said Dionysus, "unless it be of gods." "Ariadne", said Dionysus, "you are a labyrinth: Theseus has gone astray in you, he has lost the thread; of what good is it to him that he is not devoured by the Minotaur? That which devours him is worse than a Minotaur."
"You are flattering me", Ariadne replied: "I am weary of my

pity, all heroes should perish by me: this is my ultimate love for Theseus: I destroy him."

The three characters in this "satyr play" are Nietzsche (Dionysus), Wagner (Theseus) and Wagner's wife and widow, Cosima (Ariadne). If the sketch itself left any doubt as to these attributions it would be set aside by the content of the letters Nietzsche sent out to people he knew, and to prominent people he did not know, during the days following his mental collapse. Some are signed "Dionysus", and Cosima Wagner is referred to in them as "Ariadne"; one of the letters that went to Cosima herself reads: "Ariadne. I love you. Dionysus". At the clinic at Jena in which he was subsequently confined Nietzsche is recorded as having said: "My wife Cosima Wagner brought me here" – the "wedding of Dionysus and Ariadne" having by then taken place in his now uninhibited fantasy. It thus appears that the poem "Who still warms me, who still loves me?" has simply been taken away from Wagner and given to Cosima, in whose mouth it has acquired a truthfulness it could not possess in Wagner's.

Fame and Eternity (page 67)

There is some indication that "Fame and Eternity" was at first intended as a poetic epilogue to the autobiography *Ecce Homo*: this intention, if it in fact existed, would have been sensible, since this miniature poetic cycle is itself autobiographical. It records, in the concisest way, four stages on Zarathustra's path to enlightenment. Part i ("How long have you already brooded") is ferociously depressive: truth, "brimstone-coloured" and sulphurous, a curse and thunderstorm that shakes the rafters, inspires anger in him who says it and fear in those who hear it. A prose equivalent is provided in *Ecce Homo* in the characterization of *On the Genealogy of Morals*:

> The three essays of which this Genealogy consists are in regard to expression, intention and art of surprise perhaps the uncanniest things that have ever been written. Dionysus is, as one knows, also the god of darkness. – Each time a beginning

which is *intended* to mislead, cool, scientific, even ironic, intentionally foreground, intentionally keeping in suspense. Gradually an increasing disquiet; isolated flashes of lightning; very unpleasant truths becoming audible as a dull rumbling in the distance – until at last a *tempo feroce* is attained in which everything surges forward with tremendous tension. At the conclusion each time amid perfectly awful detonations a *new* truth visible between thick clouds.

Part 2 ("This coin . . .") appears to repudiate "fame", actually repudiates the purchase of fame by the substitution of virtue for truth – the trimming of truth to the world's moral demands. The third and fourth poems transport us to the end of Part Three of *Zarathustra*, the ecstatic conclusion of Zarathustra's spiritual odyssey and his attainment of full enlightenment. The euphoric imagery is here so closely compacted as sometimes to constitute almost a series of catch-words and -phrases whose meaning, though well and unequiv-ocally established in Nietzsche's earlier writings and familiar to readers of them, is by no means conveyed by the text of the poem itself. I think I shall have done my duty by the reader if I offer, not a full "explication" of this text – which would in any case probably exhaust his/her patience – but the following *key* which may by itself prove adequate to unlocking it. The passage again comes from *Ecce Homo*:

> My formula for greatness in a human being is *amor fati*: that one wants nothing to be other than it is, not in the future, not in the past, not in all eternity. Not merely to endure that which happens of necessity, still less to dissemble it – all idealism is untruthfulness in the face of necessity – but to *love* it. . . .

Of the Poverty of the Richest Man (page 75)

The last of the *Dithyrambs of Dionysus* relaxes tempo and tension. It is the happiest poem in the collection. The opening line answers the question asked by the opening lines of "Fame and Eternity" and in doing so recalls the opening of *Thus Spoke Zarathustra*:

> When Zarathustra was thirty years old, he left his home and the lake of his home and went into the mountains. Here he had the enjoyment of his spirit and his solitude and he did not weary of it for ten years. But at last his heart turned – and one morning he rose with the dawn, stepped before the sun, and spoke to it thus . . .

In the light of these correspondences, it is probably not far-fetched to conclude that the "Zarathustras" of the *Dithyrambs of Dionysus* are not so much repetitions of the grand central figure of *Thus Spoke Zarathustra* as *alternatives* to him.

Some classic German poetry from Anvil

Goethe: Roman Elegies
and other poems
TRANSLATED BY MICHAEL HAMBURGER

Johann Wolfgang von Goethe (1749–1832) is mainly known in the English-speaking world as the poet of *Faust*. His other poetry, for all its richness and variety, has received comparatively little attention. This edition collects all the versions made over many years by Michael Hamburger. His selection and introduction provide a valuable account of 'a writer so many-sided as to constitute a whole literature'. Here are poems from all periods of Goethe's creative life, including a complete version of the erotic *Roman Elegies*.

Friedrich Hölderlin: Poems and Fragments
TRANSLATED BY MICHAEL HAMBURGER

Michael Hamburger has been translating the poetry of Friedrich Hölderlin (1770–1843) for over half a century. This third edition includes many new translations and other supplementary material. It contains the greater part of Hölderlin's odes in classical metre, the most characteristic of the later elegies, all the free-verse hymns (including many fragments of hymns drafted before the poet's withdrawal from society) as well as the second and third versions of his great tragedy *Der Tod des Empedokles*. It is likely to be the standard bilingual edition of Hölderlin's poetry for many years.

"Readers of more than one generation owe a debt to Michael Hamburger as a translator. Few can have done more to enhance (and in many cases create) the appreciation of German poetry among an Anglophone audience"
> – Sean O'Brien, *Times Literary Supplement*